THE CORRESPONDENCE OF THOMAS WOLFE

AND HOMER ANDREW WATT

HOMER ANDREW WATT IN 1926

THE CORRESPONDENCE OF

THOMAS WOLFE

AND

HOMER ANDREW WATT

EDITED BY OSCAR CARGILL

AND

THOMAS CLARK POLLOCK

New York University Press

WASHINGTON SQUARE · NEW YORK

London: Geoffrey Cumberlege   Oxford University Press

1954

All of the letters from Thomas Wolfe in this volume copyright 1954 by Edward C. Aswell, Administrator C.T.A. of the Estate of Thomas Wolfe.

All of the letters from Homer Andrew Watt and the letter from Chancellor Harry Woodburn Chase and all other materials in this volume except the aforesaid letters from Thomas Wolfe copyright 1954 by New York University.

TO THE GOOD MEMORY OF

HOMER ANDREW WATT

TABLE OF CONTENTS

vii

SUPPLEMENT

INTRODUCTORY

NOTE

THOMAS WOLFE was an instructor in English in the Washington Square College of Arts and Science — then called simply Washington Square College — of New York University from February 6, 1924, to February 6, 1930.

The chairman of the Department of English in Washington Square College at that time was Professor Homer Andrew Watt.

On January 10, 1924, Thomas Wolfe, then a graduate student in Professor George Pierce Baker's 47 Workshop at Harvard University, wrote to Professor Watt asking for "employment" as a teacher of English. January was still young, and Wolfe dated the letter 1923 instead of 1924. He said that he had had no experience as a teacher and some day he hoped to write successfully for the theater and do nothing but that; but he promised that if he were offered the chance to teach English he would give "the most faithful and efficient service" of which he was capable.

Dr. Watt liked Wolfe's letter and his references and offered him an instructorship in English for the spring and summer terms of 1924 beginning on February 6 at a salary of $1,800. He also told Wolfe that he thought he would like him. This proved to be true, and in the next six years Homer Watt went well beyond the call of his duty as a departmental chairman to make it possible for Thomas Wolfe to have a teaching position when he needed one and to avoid teaching when he needed the time more. It is of course now part of the literary history of the 1920's and 1930's that during the next few years the young instructor in English — who really did give his teaching job the most faithful and efficient service of which he was capable — was primarily interested in his own urgent struggle with life and his expression of it, not so much on the stage, as he had hoped, but in *Look Homeward, Angel* and the books that followed it.

The record indicates that Wolfe taught in New York University during the spring and summer terms of 1924; the academic years 1925-1926 and 1927-1928; the spring term of 1929, and the fall term of 1929-1930. He accepted appointment as an instructor in English for the entire academic year 1929-1930 at a salary of $2,400; but *Look Homeward, Angel* was published in October 1929 and proved to be a success. Scribner's gave him an advance of $5,000 on his next book,[1] and he resigned his teaching position at the end of the fall term, 1929-1930.

Two days before Professor Watt died on October 4, 1948, in the French Hospital in New York City, he asked to see me. He told me that he regarded his relation with Thomas Wolfe as the most important part of his career as a departmental administrator; that he had kept his correspondence with Thomas Wolfe; and that he regarded this as the property of New York University. He had tried to find time to edit this correspondence and to write his own memories of Thomas Wolfe, but had been able only to begin. He wanted me to take charge of the letters and to be chairman of a committee to edit them. The committee was to include Professor Oscar Cargill and he hoped, faintly, himself. Chancellor Harry Woodburn Chase of New York University, who had known Wolfe previously at the University of North Carolina, also had kept an exchange of correspondence with him, and Dr. Watt hoped that this could be included with his own letters, the whole to be published for the benefit of a Thomas Wolfe Scholarship Fund for the study of American literature.

[1] *Thomas Wolfe's Letters to His Mother* (New York: Charles Scribner's Sons, 1943), p. 193.

The net profits from the present volume will go to the benefit of this fund.

For their help in making possible the publication of this correspondence, Professor Cargill and I wish to thank especially Mr. Edward C. Aswell, the Administrator of the Estate of Thomas Wolfe; Dr. Harry Woodburn Chase, chancellor emeritus of New York University; and Homer Andrew Watt's son, Professor William Whyte Watt.

THOMAS CLARK POLLOCK

THE WOLFE-WATT CORRESPONDENCE

Cambridge, Mass.

January 10, 1923 [1924]

Dear Professor Watt: I am informed that there will be several vacancies in the English department at New York University on the opening of the new term, in February. I have requested the Harvard Appointment Bureau to forward my papers, including letters and scholastic grades, to you. Mr Dow,[1] formerly of Harvard, and now an instructor at the uptown branch of the university, may also be consulted.

I was graduated, as you will note, from the University of North Carolina, in 1920, and received my master's degree, in English, from Harvard, in 1922. The appointment office secured me an offer from Northwestern University in 1922, which I ultimately refused in order to return for another year under Professor Baker at the 47 Workshop. Thus, I have been a student in the Graduate School for three years.

I have had no experience as a teacher. It is only fair to tell you that my interests are centered in the drama, and that someday I hope to write successfully for the theatre and to do nothing but that. My play is at present in the hands of a producer in New York but, even in the fortunate event of its acceptance, I feel the necessity of finding immediate employment.

I am twenty three years old and a native of Asheville, North Carolina. I do not know what impression of maturity my appearance may convey but it is hardly in excess of my age. In addition, my height is four or five inches over six feet, producing an effect on a stranger that is sometimes startling. I think you should know so much in advance, as these considerations may justly enter into any estimates of my qualifications.

If New York University feels justified in offering me employment as an instructor in English, and if I am satisfied with the offer, I promise to give the most faithful and efficient service of which I am capable.

I hope you will find it convenient to reply to this letter at some early date.

Faithfully yours,

Thomas Wolfe

10 Trowbridge St
Cambridge, Mass.

---

[1]Robert B. Dow was a member of the English Department, University College ("the uptown branch"), from 1923 to 1926, and of the same department in Washington Square College from 1926 until his death in 1953. He became Associate Professor of English and Assistant Director of Admissions.

All persons mentioned in these letters are further identified in *Thomas Wolfe at Washington Square*, New York University Press, 1954.

NEW YORK UNIVERSITY

WASHINGTON SQUARE COLLEGE

WASHINGTON SQUARE, NEW YORK

DEPARTMENT OF ENGLISH

January 13, 1924

Mr. Thomas Clayton Wolfe,
10 Trowbridge Street,
Cambridge, Massachusetts.

My dear Mr. Wolfe:

I like your letter, and from what your professors and friends have said about you, I think that I shall like you too. At any rate I am now offering you an instructorship in the Washington Square College of New York University for the two terms from February 6 to September 1 or thereabouts, at a salary of $1800 for the full period. If you wish to accept, please let me know at once, as I must fill the position before the first of next month.

You have been frank with me, and I will be equally frank with you. First, a word about the position. The New York City high schools graduate large classes about February 1. Many of these students wish to enter college immediately, and to accommodate them we offer freshman subjects spread over spring and summer in such a way that those taking the full course catch up with the September crowd by the September following their February entrance. That is, the course which I am inviting you to give is divided into two semesters, the first ending about June 1, the second about September 1. I should expect you to accept work for this full period. Payments for February to September instructors are divided into eight parts; that is, you would receive eight payments of $225 each, the first on March 1 and the last on October 1. Your work, however, will certainly be over about the middle of September. Appointments are made for one academic year, but are subject to renewal. The instructors who teach from February to September, however, do not renew their teaching until the following February.

In September, instructors who have not at least an M. A. and some experience in college teaching are rarely appointed. In February, however, exceptions are sometimes made. This February we shall have eight new instructors, most of whom are experienced men. Some of these teachers, however, are not planning to continue in university work, but are training themselves as writers; and I place you in this category.

You will find yourself in a congenial crowd of eager young men. Your friend Dow is at University Heights, but Bruce Carpenter,[1] who knows you, is teaching on the down-town staff, and you and he will have much to talk about, for he too is trying to launch a dramatic ship on the troubled stream of Broadway.

You will teach three sections — about ninety students — how to make sentences and paragraphs. You will probably learn more from them than they will from you, but I have a feeling that you will get along well with them. You will find them rough but eager, and such students are not difficult to handle. Your weekly program will be from eight to ten hours besides some office and conference hours. I shall also expect you to help with the student advisory system, but you will not have so many advisees that this work will be a burden. Mr. Carpenter and the rest will be glad to give you suggestions.

You should report for work during the week of January 28, if possible; lectures for the new term begin on February 6.

Very truly yours,

H. A. Watt
Professor of English

---

[1] Bruce Carpenter, at present Associate Professor of English in Washington Square College, came to the department in 1920. Like Wolfe, he was a product of George Pierce Baker's 47 Workshop course in the drama at Harvard.

WESTERN UNION TELEGRAM

3:18 P. M.

Jan. 21, 1924

Accept instructorship will report Feb first will you acknowledge wire.

Thomas Wolfe

November the eighteenth

1 9 2 4

Mr. Thomas C. Wolfe
48 Spruce Street
Asheville
North Carolina

My dear Mr. Wolfe:

Before you left you did not let me know definitely, as I remember it, whether or not you wished to be considered an applicant for an instructorship in English from February to September, 1925. I am now making up my staff for this division of the department and should like to offer you an appointment at the salary of $2000 which is an increase of $200 over what you received last year. You will have the usual program of three sections of freshman English.

The appointment runs officially from February, 1924 to February, 1925 and the salary is paid in twelve parts each one of which is paid on the first of each month. The Bursar's Office is eager to have me notify February instructors that there can be no departure from this method of dividing the salaries.

Will you please let me know at once whether you can accept the appointment and will be with us in February?

Cordially yours,

H. A. Watt
Professor of English

HAW/B

My mailing address is American Express Co. Paris.

Letter will be forwarded.

AMERICAN EXPRESS

The American Express Co., Inc.   Visitor's Writing Room

11, Rue Scribe   (not official)

Paris......Jan. 15..........1925

Dear Professor Watt:— I am conscious that the letter I promised to write you has been long delayed; I shall tell you the extraordinary reasons for the delay.

I have had an astonishing voyage — I spent 1 month in England, went down about every back alley in London, and into most of the disreputable pubs; about six weeks ago I came to Paris and settled in a small hotel in the Latin Quarter.

I went to this place with my bags very late at night — one o'clock — the concierge who admitted me had been wounded in the war, and gave a great groan when he saw the baggage, and when I told him my room was five flights up, He pointed to his crippled leg, and hobbled around painfully; I suggested that he keep one of the bags until morning. I would take the other two myself. He agreed to this gladly; the story is that during the night a man entered, asked for a woman formerly [resident?] of the hotel, and on the way out stole my bag.

The bag was old and battered, the articles in it were not of great value; what it did contain that could not be replaced was the prolog and two acts in manuscript of the play I had lived with for more than a year.

I know it sounds silly, but nothing has hit me like this since the death of my brother Ben six years ago. I moved to another hotel the next day; I bought paper and swore that I should rewrite the play in two weeks — by New Year's — and on January 3 I had not only re-created what was lost, but completed an entire first draft. Since then I have been re-writing.

For three weeks I saw or spoke practically to no one; then I met friends, and have passed the time very pleasantly since. Good or bad, what I have done in these past five weeks is the best I have ever done. I am rather glad the thing was stolen; it has helped me.

The hotel people, after a very nasty scene, paid me 500 francs for the loss of the valise: they suggested it was a conspiracy (which they knew to be false), and I told them they were dishonest scoundrels — after I got my fingers on the 500.

Since very charming friends — including two attractive ladies — have purchased a car, and want me to go South with them for two or three months. I think I shall do this.

You spoke to me early about the February term; later you suggested that the matter was uncertain, because of large enrollment and so on. At any rate, although my own money is nearly gone, I feel that everything that is happening to me now is too important to be checked violently; I shall stay over, if possible, some months longer; my mother, I believe, will help me.

In five weeks time I have acquired enough French to read very easily — and to speak very badly, but comprehensibly, without the necessity of beginning all over. I am entering a new world of art and letters; during the past two weeks I have been to some incredible places — working men's dance halls; all night lodgings where the wretches are huddled in sleep, a hundred to a room, over long tables, drugged by their own weariness, and by the overpowering stench of the bodies; breathing as one like a great terrible organ

If I didn't make it sufficiently plain before I left, let me emphasize now the gratitude and affection I bear toward you for your kindliness, patience, and forbearance last year — for me, just hatching out, a genuine anno mirabalis

When I come back I shall certainly be in to see you; if you only have time, meanwhile, to write me a line or two, you would give me a great deal of delight and pleasure.

If this seems to you to be hastily scribbled by a man coming out of a dream, I think your intuition will be correct. But I'm all right now, and beginning to live.

With best cordial regards,

Tom Wolfe

· V I ·

February the twenty-fourth

1 9 2 5

Mr. Thomas Wolfe
American Express Company, Inc.
11 Rue Scribe
Paris, France

My dear Mr. Wolfe:

I was glad to hear from you last month but sorry that you found it impossible to be with us this semester. You apparently did not receive the letter which I sent to your American address last November which contained an offer of an instructorship for the February-September term at $2000. Inasmuch as I had not heard from you I had turned in your name to the Committee and your appointment had been approved. Your letter indicating, therefore, that you were not returning was somewhat of a surprise to me and made me hustle to get a man for your position. I finally appointed Mr. Terry,[1] a North Carolina man whom you probably know and who will probably take your place.

In a way I am not at all sorry that you did not return this February inasmuch as it gives me an opportunity to offer you a position as instructor on the regular September-June staff. This would be at the figure which I have already mentioned, $2000. If you care to accept the appointment, will you please let me know at once in order that I may not be put in the same position that I found myself in in regard to your other position. I assure you that I should be very glad to have your favorable response inasmuch as I should like to have you working with us on the regular staff here. Your program would consist of the freshman composition and sophomore literature.

I quite envy you your good time. I have not seen nearly as much of France as you have but what I did see of Paris and northern France gave me a taste for more. Your ability to land on your feet in spite of whatever misfortune you may encounter makes me think that you are more like a Thomas cat than a Thomas Wolfe. Don't let the ladies run away with you. Up to a certain extent playing the part of lecturer to ladies in Paris may give you training in handling co-eds successfully here, but two of my instructors who flitted to Paris last year came back under petticoat government and I begin to fear the country and its effects upon confirmed young bachelors. The ladies, I know, have somewhat of a feeling for you. I remember your friend poor little _____ _____² and the impression which she and her mother gave the entire hotel guest room when she did her best to weep you into a higher grade. Incidentally, it may please you to know that _____ _____'s² days here are at a definite end. It didn't take the Scholarship Committee long to come to the conclusion that_____ _____² has bran for brains, but it did take some time to convince_____ _____² of the fact. I think, however, that we have succeeded in convincing the entire _____² family that Washington Square College is no place for her, and I promise you that if you return here you need have no further fear that the sanctity of your quarters at the Hotel Albert would be invaded.

Please do come back, Wolfe. Since you left we have had no one to keep the elevator boys in their proper places and we miss your diminutive form in the faculty room. Send me a letter special delivery and say "Thanks, I'll be back". Mr. Munn is not here but I know that if he were he would send you his best regards, and with that message I will sign off for this time.

Yours sincerely,

H. A. Watt

HAW/T

<hr>

[1] John Skally Terry, a friend of Wolfe from North Carolina undergraduate days, is the editor of *Thomas Wolfe's Letters to His Mother* and was at the time of his death in 1953 Assistant Professor of English in Washington Square College.

[2] Name of student deleted.

St. Raphaël

[April, 1925]

Dear Professor Watt:—

I am sending you a hasty scrawl here in answer to your letter of several weeks ago, but I shall follow with another of a more explanatory nature   I want to get this off on the day's mail. I am on the Riviera, in a little town posessed mainly by the English, and I am writing as if pursued by devils. This will perhaps show in my writing.

Let me say here that if I were methodical enough to keep a scrap book your last letter would occupy a position of honor in it. I am very proud of it; proud and pleased to know that I am wanted for something and that I am worth as much as $2000 to anyone.

I was in Tours when your letter came to Paris — my mail was being held for me, and I did not get your letter for several weeks. I departed almost at once for the South of France.

First of all, I am terribly shocked at the confusion that resulted when I did not return. I did *not* get your earlier letter offering me a place in February; you say that you sent it to my "American address", and I have wondered whether you meant the Albert, or Asheville, N.C. If you sent it to Asheville, it should have been forwarded by my brother, although my mother closed her house and departed for Miami early in the Fall.

Today I heard from home, and my family is evidently desirous that I return in August. I am therefore writing you to tell you that I

they seem to have a touching belief
in me without knowing very well what
I am doing. And what I am doing is
to write, write, write — it may be
the most frightful muck, but I can't
help putting it down. At times
I grow slightly bitter at the idea
of having to stop writing, even temporarily,
to do something of a more profitable
character. I feel at such a time that
my own destiny has been matched against
that of a piece of black earth in
Carolina, and a piece of sand in Florida,
and that the land always wins.

At the same time there is another
impulse in me which makes me

"THE LAND ALWAYS WINS"

A page from Wolfe's penciled letter from St. Raphaël in April 1925.

accept with the deepest gratitude your offer of a post in September.

You have always shown the utmost patience with me, Professor Watt, even in circumstances where my greenness must have been excessively trying to your patience and good nature. But I have had one instinct towards you that has been a happy and a right one; I have never had the slightest hesitation in speaking to you in absolute honesty, without concealment that is why I am going to give you certain information now about my domestic background and my present circumstances which I feel it is necessary you should have, in order to understand my present state of mind.

My mother is a very extraordinary woman in her middle sixties, small, strong, intensely vigorous, and uncannily canny in business affairs; she is part Scotch. Since my father's death a few years ago she has, by shrewd investment at home and in Florida, more than trebled her estate. For every cent I spend I am, at the present time, absolutely dependent on my mother.

I spent the few thousand dollars that came to me following my father's death at Harvard. My other brother's and sisters following my mother's advice, have profited hugely. And everyone, you understand, has been beautifully loyal to me They seem to have a touching belief in me without knowing very well what I am doing. And what I am doing is to write, write, write — it may be the most frightful muck, but I can't help putting it down. At times I grow slightly bitter at the idea of having to stop writing, even temporarily, to do something of a more profitable character. I feel at such a time that my own destiny has been matched against that of a piece of black earth in Carolina, and a piece of sand in Florida, and that the land always wins.

At the same time there is another impulse in me which makes me rather fiercely independent; I have a horror of becoming like those wretched little rats at Harvard who are at the mercy of their pangs and quivers, who whine about their "art", who whine that the world has not given them a living. I'll be damned if I'll become a "chronic unemployable"

It was this that Professor Baker could not understand; he protested that I was making a serious blunder in coming to the university, he seemed absolutely unable to comprehend my reasons, he said "You must keep on writing", and he kept on saying this with a sublime disregard for circumstances. I settled the business for myself — the only possible settlement, as I found — and I lost, I fear, the friendship of a man who had stood by me for two years; at any rate, I have never heard from him.

That is why, even now, I doubt; and that is why I seem to hesitate. I observe a rather widespread tendency among older people to condemn the conduct of young people as headstrong and obstinate, but I do not observe a widespread tendency to give a plain answer to some of the questions young people ask.

I should like to think, frankly, that something I have written or am writing might in these next few months relieve me of the necessity of doing anything else. I keep hoping for a little more time, but I know that you need time as well. You may be assured, however, that, my word being given, I will come through to the scratch, death or disease excepted.

And I want to repeat what I believe you already know; for innumerable reasons I prefer to be at N.Y.U. to any other place North or South   There is, at the present time, one possible means for me to keep on with my work. If it is not too late, will you drop me a line, and let me know how much time for further meditation you can allow me? I beg of you not to be too impatient at what seems to be my indecision; — I am in a web of tangled and troubling event, only the barest outlines of which I have been able to indicate to you. I hope you have not been bored with the recital

I am reading French like a streak; and I have had a series of bizarre and amusing adventures. I fell into the clutches — in a thoroughly

Episcopal fashion, I assure you — of an aged Countess at Orléans, a countess who drinks horse's blood to revive her fainting spirits, and if I ever get the thing on paper, true to the mark, I'm made.

I am living here in a land of opulent Springtime, of incredible color. I should like to tell you more about it, but I'm not sure its really true. My address continues at the American Express Co, Paris. Mail will be forwarded. I go from here to Italy, then to England.

Meanwhile, I am, with the most cordial regards

Faithfully yours

Tom Wolfe

April the twentieth

1 9 2 5

Mr. Thomas Wolfe
American Express Company, Inc.
11 Rue Scribe
Paris, France

My dear Mr. Wolfe:

Sometime ago I wrote to you offering you an instructorship in English for the regular school year September-June 1925-1926, at a salary of $2000. I asked that you reply at once in order that I might be sure that you could be with us next year. So far I have heard nothing from you and am again urging you to let me have your decision. I should appreciate it very much if you could cable to me the single word "Yes" if you can be with us, or "No" if you cannot. Please let me know. I am sending a duplicate letter to your southern address.

Sincerely yours,

H. A. Watt

HAW/T

May the sixth

1 9 2 5

Mr. Thomas Wolfe
c/o American Express Company
Paris, France

My dear Wolfe:

I have read with very much interest and pleasure your pencilled
letter from St. Raphaël. I think that I can understand some of your
difficulties and shall do what I can to serve as father confessor and
help you out.

I presume that persons like yourself who have the thirst for writing will always feel that unless they allow their ruling passion to con-
trol them completely, they will be wasting their time. Naturally you
do not want to pick up sticks and straws when you might be chasing
a rainbow. I readily understand, I think, just why Professor Baker
was afraid that if you got into my clutches, as you did into the horse
blood drinking countess; I might use your razor-like mind for whit-
tling out my perfectly wooden freshmen and spoil you for all higher
purposes. Carpenter's experience here, if Mr. Baker knew about it,
would convince him that I am entirely aware of the danger of dead-
ening a man's creative impulses by grinding them off on freshman
English sections, but Professor Baker does not know this and he does
not know, moreover, that I do not take toward my department the
average administrator's attitude. This I say in all due modesty. I believe that there is room in a department, especially in New York

City, not only for excellent teachers and good scholars, but for men who have a creative impulse. Indeed, I have a feeling that the department can absorb with profit a reasonable number of temperamental gentlemen like yourself who have color and imagination to inspire students as well as to teach them. If I did not think this true I should certainly not have invited you to join our group. I do not believe that your experience in the February-September division last year resulted in your feeling that you had been entirely crowded down. Indeed, from what Miss Eggleston and others of your friends tell me you seem to have got a good deal of a "kick" out of the contact of your work as well as some feeling of independence in earning your own living. I feel perfectly sure that Carpenter's experience has been the same. I have a feeling that in giving himself out here and stimulating earnest students to creative work he reaps a great deal of inspiration which may be translated into terms of creative effort. He has been unusually active this year and has written a play and a novel and a half and as far as I can see his teaching has not only not suffered as a result but has been the better.

I do not wish to urge you against your inclination to accept the appointment here because if you come unwillingly, your work would suffer unconsciously from your adverse attitude. I do have a feeling however, that you will find the work here stimulating rather than otherwise and, of course, since appointments are only for one year, there is no reason why you should not cut loose almost at any time that you like. Association in the department here is like a trial marriage which can be annulled almost at will and without any of the disrepute that comes from divorce in social circles. My suggestion would be, therefore, that you make up your mind to try it for a year, especially since your program will be pleasanter in the September-June division than it was in the other, and that if you find that the teaching puts an end to all creative impulse and capacity, you resign at the end of the year.

I do not remember whether or not I told you in an earlier letter that I am to be on a leave of absence next year and shall spend my time at the University of Southern California, Los Angeles. Professor Munn[1] will be chairman of the department and will be your chief for the year. I know that you will find contact with him very stimulating and that you will enjoy working with the interesting group of instructors who are now with us. Two of your future confreres are now in Paris, by the way, and you will probably not meet them until after you get here. I am not going to try to forward any more letters. The letters which were lost went to Ashville and were, apparently, never sent to you.

Under separate cover, I am sending you a bulletin which will give you the calendar for next year. If you have any preferences as to teaching hours, please let me know.

Very cordially yours,

H. A. Watt

HAW/T

---

[1] James Buell Munn, since 1932 Professor of English in Harvard University, where he received his academic training, came to New York University as an instructor in 1920 and rose to be Professor of English and Dean of Washington Square College before his resignation in 1932.

Brasserie Vetzel
1 Rue Auber
Place de L'Opéra — Paris

June 22, '25

Dear Professor Watt:—

I went to Italy almost immediately after receiving your last letter; and I have been travelling and living with one valise. Since, returning to Paris only a day or two ago. I shall go back to America in August, and want to spend a few weeks at home before returning to the University. I believe the date of the term's opening is around September 20, and that you want, generally, the instructors to return a little in advance.

If the request is not extravagant will you absolve me from this preliminary work of registration? I desire this solely because of the exigencies of time.

You asked me my preferences concerning hours. I have none, save a prejudice against nine o'clocks. I am incurably and unfortunately night-owlish, doing a good part of my work when most of the world, even in New York, is silent; getting Satanic inspirations from the dark.

I think you will understand that I express something stronger than a perfunctory regret when I tell you that I am profoundly sorry to hear that you will be absent next year. My decision to return was not utterly contingent on your own presence, but it was considerably strengthened by the expectation of again working with you.

I await with great pleasure my association with Professor Munn.

Italy was for me the core of the world's loveliness; and this I take to be a miraculous thing, because that great current which draws some men toward the Latins does not draw me, who have fog in my soul, and think grey the best of colours, and London the most unfathomable of cities.

I stayed there until my money was gone; and I ended at last in Venice, which I shall remember not as a place which may always be reached by train, but as one of those cities that never were, formed in magic by the sweep of a wizard's arm.

I am going to England in a day or so, and I shall remain there for the remainder of my time. If you have any further communications, I suggest that you send them to the American Express Co., London. I wrote you before in pencil because I had no ink; I write you now upon the only paper provided by Vetzel's; it is used, generally, I believe, by young men and women naming a time and place. This is no reason why it should not Serve a worthier Purpose.

I am thoroughly disreputable in appearance, I have no clothes, and I shall have none until more money comes from home. At the present moment I am drinking nothing stronger than beer; there is, five feet away, a Frenchman, all whiskers, with a glowing cigarette tip blooming dangerously in the midst of the foliage, an old man and his young mistress just beyond, two Americans drinking cognac across, and an amorous couple at the back, kissing each other with solid smacks between draughts of beer.

I've done my best to give you a picture of Parisian life.

Faithfully yours,

Tom Wolfe

July the sixteenth

1 9 2 5

Mr. Thomas Wolfe

c/o American Express Company

London, England

My dear Mr. Wolfe:

I have your letter written from Paris and hasten to reply in order
that you may receive word before leaving London. Your request to
be relieved of attendance during registration days is reasonable
under the circumstances and you need not report, therefore, until
September 21. Recitations begin on Tuesday, September 22. As I
had not heard from you regarding hours, I had to go ahead and work
out your schedule by guess. I have managed, however, by what you
may consider an intuitional judgment of your desires to give you a
program which comes entirely in the afternoon. I mailed you a
schedule and my annual "pastoral" letter regarding the work for
next year, but it is quite possible that these sheets have not reached
you. Accordingly, I append here your program:

English	1-2 (D)	M.W.F.	2-3
"	1-2 (M)	M.W.F.	3-4
"	1-2 (D)	M.W.F.	5-6
"	110.3-4	Th.	4.15-6

The first three of these courses are the freshman English, nine
hours in all; the fourth is a course in introduction to literature for
teachers. You will find that many of these ladies are older than you,

but don't be frightened. I feel certain that they will take you to their collective bosoms and will listen gladly to the words of literary wisdom which you patter forth upon them. Mr. Carpenter quite enjoys teaching this particular group and I have always found the work pleasant in spite of the fact that it is often necessary to dynamite the gentle creatures into a state of receptivity.

As the time approaches for my departure westward, I find that I regret breaking off association with the men here. I know, however, that you will enjoy working with Mr. Munn and that you will get a great deal of stimulation from renewed contact with Carpenter and with other men in the department. You will find that the staff has grown almost beyond recognition in the brief time since your departure.

You will be very fond of Professor McCullough,[1] who has immediate charge of freshman English and who is a corking fellow all round. I lifted him from the chairmanship of the department at Chattanooga last year and have never for a minute regretted the act.

Carpenter brought back a mustache from his vacation, and last year Hoffmann and Loggins[2] brought back wives from theirs. What will you bring? You will understand, of course, that the department requires neither.

My best good wishes to you for a pleasant sojourn in the gray city on the Thames and an enjoyable and safe return to America.

Cordially yours,

H. A. Watt

---

[1] Bruce McCullough, a native of Indiana, took his doctorate at the University of Pennsylvania, served in the American Army in France, and taught in two other institutions before coming to New York University. He has edited novels by Jane Austen and Thomas Hardy and written important criticism in the field of fiction.

[2] Harold Hoffmann and Vernon Loggins, instructors in the College; the former has since died; the latter is teaching at Columbia.

· XII ·

NEW YORK UNIVERSITY

WASHINGTON SQUARE COLLEGE

MEMORANDUM TO Mr. Wolfe:

Date: January 3, 1927

    I should like to see you regarding a possible appointment in the Department of English.

Cordially yours,

H. A. Watt
Administrative Chairman

:B

February the fifth

1 9 2 7

Mr. Thomas Wolfe
Harvard Club
27 West 44 Street
New York City

My dear Wolfe:

The list of applicants for the English Department vacancies for next year has been so full and the quality of the applications so thoroughly satisfactory that about the only way that I could make sure about holding a place for you was to recommend your appointment on the regular budget with the expectation that you would accept the position. Accordingly, Dean Turner [1] approved my recommendation of your appointment as instructor in English, Washington Square College, for 1927-1928 at a salary of $2200. This, as you know, is $200 more than you had when you taught here last and is the figure which I should have given you if you had accepted the February to September appointment.

I suggest that you accept this appointment in order that you may be sure of a good position for next year. If not later than the first of May you find that it will be impossible for you to be with us next year, please let me know promptly in order that I may appoint another instructor in your place. I need hardly say that if I wanted you to do this, I should hardly have recommended you on my first budget list.

I should appreciate a prompt letter of acceptance to this letter since I am eager to have my department for next year stabilized at an early date. Please drop in and see us from time to time.

Cordially yours,

H. A. Watt
Administrative Chairman

:B

---

[1] John Roscoe Turner, economist, was Dean of Washington Square College from 1917 to 1928. Later he was President of West Virginia University and Dean of Men in the City College of New York.

Hotel Hemenway
Boston
Leonard H. Torrey

Monday Night
March 7, 1927

Dear Professor Watt:— I have come to Boston for a few days to see
some friends and to get several dozen volumes of divine poetry, relics
of my youth, which, in a foolish moment, I left with my uncle three
years ago. The opportunities for forcible entry and a bit of high
grade burglary are especially good; Handsome Henry,[1] bereft of
his first a year ago, is at present enjoying his seventy fourth year in
Florida with his second, a blooming lass of thirty.

I have besought the old philanthropist repeatedly to send me my
books. I even gave him money for freight, and I have been fed on
oily evasions. Tomorrow, accompanied by one of his none too obedi-
ent daughters, I shall try direct action. I know the effort will carry
your blessing.

I had your letter several weeks ago; I have thought it over many
times. Later, Carlton[2] told me that he had talked with you, and that
you suggested that I accept the appointment to teach next September, with the understanding that I might withdraw my acceptance
provided I informed you within reasonable time.

I know you will be glad to hear that I have worked hard and
steadily in my garret, and that I hope to have my huge book on
paper by May, and in the hands of a publisher (I hope!) by summer.
I think you understand that what I want to do with my life is to live

by and for my writing. That independence — I had better say that slavery — is the highest desire I have ever known. To hope for it at present is precarious. I thank you again, fervently, for your patience, your kindness, and your encouragement. May I assume that if the miracle (of publication and royalty) does not happen, I can have employment in the September division, and if it does, and I am able to go on under my own steam, that I may decently (before the term's beginning) withdraw?

I am returning to New York day after tomorrow. My mail address is still the Harvard Club. I shall come in to see you during the month.

Life is many days. But I'm at a time when it seems very short. My twenty-six years weigh on me and, rather desperately, I feel my lack of achievement. I surrender myself again, therefore, to your extra-ordinary indulgence, which has been unfailing.

Faithfully yours,

Thomas Wolfe

This is a bad, groping, fumbling letter. I've said what I wanted to say, but badly. I've been roaming over Concord all day and climbing the tower in Hawthorne's house. I'm tired.

[1] An uncle of Thomas Wolfe.

[2] Henry Carlton, friend of Wolfe, was also a 47 Workshop man. Before going into radio, he was Instructor in English in Washington Square College.

· X V ·

6 June, 1927

Mr. Thomas Wolfe
Harvard Club
27 West 44 Street
New York City

My dear Mr. Wolfe:

Under separate cover, I am sending you a copy of the Washington Square College bulletin for next year which contains descriptions of our courses in English. Inasmuch as copy for this bulletin went to press before you were appointed, it is probable that you will not find your name listed in the faculty directory. This omission has nothing to do, of course, with your appointment.

I am expecting very soon to prepare the teaching schedules for all instructors. These I should like to arrange as far as possible to suit the convenience of members of the department. I am asking, therefore, that if you have any preference for hours, you will let me know promptly. If I do not hear from you on this subject, I shall assume that you have no special requests. You will understand, of course, that the administration of the department is not absolutely free in making out these schedules, but has to fit the programs into the plan dictated by the Curriculum and Rooms Committees. It will not be possible, therefore, to grant all requests for special consideration but as far as is reasonable, I shall give the instructors programs which are satisfactory to them. The ordinary practice in making out programs is to group recitations and allow instructors at least one day a week entirely free from teaching.

33

Will you please send me also your summer address? This is important inasmuch as I shall want to send you not only your teaching schedule for next year but other announcements concerning your work. I shall be in New York City until the middle of August and shall be glad to confer during the summer with any of the new instructors who happen to be here. Any communications should be addressed to me at my office.

Dean Bouton[1] has told me of the letter which he sent to you recently. If it is your purpose to register for the conference course in College English Instruction, will you please let me know in order that I may have at an early date information concerning the enrollment in this course. I shall be glad to know also what courses, if any, you are planning to take in the Graduate School of New York University. This is simply for my own information. Concerning these courses and your registration in them, you should communicate with Dean A. L. Bouton.

Cordially yours,

H. A. Watt
Administrative Chairman

:B

---

[1]Dean Archibald L. Bouton, of the University College of New York University, was also Professor of English and head of the department.

6 June, 1927

Mr. Thomas Wolfe
Harvard Club
27 West 44 Street
New York City

My dear Mr. Wolfe:

The accompanying letter is a form letter sent to new instructors and merely mailed to you for your information.

Cordially yours,

H. A. Watt
Administrative Chairman

:B

July 25, 1927

Mr. Thomas Wolfe
Harvard Club
27 West 44th Street
New York City

My dear Mr. Wolfe:

Another of our instructors for next year, Mr. Henry Adams,[1] has kindly consented to an adjustment in his program which enables me to give you his evening hours and free your program on Fridays. This gives you really an ideal program. I cannot, of course, undertake to change it any further since it is practically impossible to adjust one program without changing at least one other.

My best wishes for a pleasant vacation.

Cordially yours,

H. A. Watt

---

[1] Henry Adams was Instructor in English in Washington Square College from 1929 to 1931.

Vienna — Aug. 11, 1927

Dear Professor Watt: — This is just a line of greeting and a re-
minder of our conversation several weeks ago about my schedule. I
hope you have finally managed (from the distressing network of
schedules you have had to arrange) to give me the hours you thought
possible. By this arrangement, I would have night classes M. T. W.
Thurs; my free time would be lumped together — highly desirable
to me.

I have been in this charming town of Vienna for two days; I came
on from Munich and the Bavarian mountains. There was a revolu-
tion here three weeks ago in which four hundred people lost their
lives but you could not tell it now from the gaiety of the city's life.
These people seem to belong to an entirely different civilization
from the Germans. There is a lightness, a delicacy, and a charm in
the life here which is as un-Teutonic as anything can be. The whole
town is much more French in its appearance — a smaller Paris, but
I believe the gaiety of the people is more spontaneous than that of
the Parisian — there is a much more honest cordiality here; they
lack the very bad Gallic hardness.

I am going from here to Prague, and from there back to Paris. I
expect to sail for New York about Sept. 10. This has been a quiet
and very rich little voyage. I am learning the German language in
gluttonous gobs and buying books with both hands. Do you know
that I talk German to these people — very bad, clumsy, halty German, it's true, but they understand me. I have very little facility for
speaking a language well, but I have a real talent for understanding

it and soaking it up. I can now speak French with a bad fluency and read and understand it as well as English. Before another year has gone by I'm going to do the same for German. Then I'm going to get Italian. It's simply fascinating to be sunk in a new language and to have the names of all the things you want — tobacco, soap, matches, veal cutlets, and so on — printed and spoken around you in a new tongue. In this way it soaks in through the pores of your skin.

The papers are terribly excited here (and all over Europe) about the Sacco-Vanzetti case. The entire front page is given to it. There seems to be a universal demand for the pardon of the men. I do not know enough about the case; I think it is likely the men *may* be guilty, but I think also the trial was long, fumbling, and prejudiced. The great pity is that a thing like this suddenly coalesces and *symbolizes,* so to speak, the terribly bitter feeling that is felt for America throughout the world today. I am finishing this letter, by the way, several days after I began it; I have been in Vienna almost a week, and the [luxurious?] charm of the place has invaded me. When I come again, I'm coming here for several months to get the language. Munich was a magnificent town, with some of the greatest things in it I've ever seen — but there's simply no changing it; there *is* a sort of German-young gentlemen with dueling scars on their faces, and older ones with shaven bullet heads, small porky eyes, and three ridges of neck over the back of their collars that I do not, I do not like! I [?] over carefully and quietly on the pavements until I found that these gentlemen had an unhappy (and I believe unconscious) habit of taking not only the four yards which was theirs, but the eight inches which was mine. All that I had ever felt about the sacredness of liberty and the rights of men boiled over, I kept grimly on my way, increased my stride just as I got upon the startled Hun, before he could retreat. God forgive me for this mean-ness of spirit; let me assure you that my prejudice, if I had any, was in their favor, because of the war's vicious propaganda. They are a very powerful and energetic people, quite ignorant, I believe, of their unpleasant qualities; they have tremendous creative and intellectual power; huge, profound, murky, and earth-shaking (like Kant and Wagner), but they are lacking in the fine delicacy and urbanity of these Viennese.

I've got to end abruptly. I hope you've had a pleasant summer. Please get me the schedule, if you can.

Faithfully yours,

Tom Wolfe

Sunday, Aug. 14.

August 31, 1927.

Mr. Thomas Wolfe,
The Harvard Club,
New York City.

Dear Mr. Wolfe:

Thanks for your fine letter of August 11th from Vienna.

I adjusted your schedule through the courtesy of Mr. Henry Adams, one of the new instructors, and your courses are now arranged as you requested in our interview. I mailed a copy of your new schedule to the Harvard Club and requested that they forward it since I thought the clerk there would have your most recent address.

The general notice which I sent to the department calls the first department meeting on Monday, September 19th. Instruction begins on the day following.

I have just returned from two weeks' absence and find my desk stacked with letters to be answered. Pardon this brief note.

Cordially yours,

H. A. Watt

j

HARVARD CLUB

27 WEST 44TH STREET

April 1, 1928

Dear Professor Watt: I am writing you this letter before I speak
to you, because I feel you may want a formal record for your files.

After long consideration I have decided not to accept a teaching
appointment at the university for next year. I think the time has
come when I must make a bold venture with my life: in some way —
not, I am afraid, very clearly defined yet — I want to get the energy of
my life directed towards the thing it desires most. In short, I am
going to try to support myself by writing — if necessary, by hack
writing of any sort, stories, advertising, articles — but *writing* of a
sort. If my book should be accepted I should, of course, immediately
start work on a new one. I know this is a gamble, but it occurs to me
that we can afford to gamble once or twice in an effort to get at the
heart of our desire. The most reckless people, I believe, are those
who never gamble at all.

During the last few days, in the tragic misfortune of Mr. Powell,[1]
I have seen again the splendid generosity which shows that New
York University is not simply a group of buildings with elevators.
And since an action of this sort must come from men, and not from
brick and stone, I am inclined to place the credit for it where I have
myself the deepest cause for gratefulness — with you and with Dr.
Munn.

I have been more tired this Spring than at any other time of my life — I have felt, along with the finishing of my book, such dam-nable weariness of my brain and heart as I did not know existed. And often, I am afraid, I have been surly, ill-tempered, unable to join happily with other people. For this, if I can not plead justifica-tion, I can at least ask pardon. But there is one assurance I must give you: once or twice, when I was in a chafed and bitter temper, I have heard some of the young men say that I occupied the position of a privileged character — that I was the departmental "wild oat", and any laxity or extravagance would be permitted me. Now this, I am sure, was harmless joking, but it touched rawly on me at the time. I think no one knows better than I do my deficiencies as a teacher — among which I would name a lack of orderly arrange-ment, an extravagant and useless expenditure of energy on all things, and a constant belief in miracles — but please believe that within my limits I have given you honest and faithful service.

It is perhaps childish for me to mention this, but I am childishly proud of this — that being notorious for a lack of discipline and reg-ularity when I came here I have, in my three years, missed only one class. That happened my first year, and was caused by the lateness of a boat returning from Boston. And I think I have never put a grade on a student's paper without trying to add a few lines of sensible and honest criticism. If you have ever had cause to doubt that I think a very simple investigation would bear me out.

Will you please understand, Professor Watt, that I am not crying myself up vainly and boastfully? Most earnestly I want you to know, now that I'm leaving, that I have not tried to pose as a Bohemian or a temperamental fellow in order to get out of work — within the trap of my nature I have done all things I could do to fulfill my obliga-tion to you. It would cause me very real distress to think you doubted that. I have been at times a very difficult, a very moody and extravagant person, but I do not believe I have been a cheap or com-mon person.

I think one of the chief reasons for my leaving now is not that I dislike teaching, and find it dull, but that I may like it too well. I find that it takes from me the same energy that I put into creation; if this is true, and there is anything in me worth saving or having, I draw comfort from the belief that my classes must have got some of the best of me during my three years.

This is a bad and clumsy letter from a tired man. But none the less it comes from a very deep place in me. Three years of my life have been spent here. I know that they have carved a mark and left a deposit. Let me assure you that I will never forget your kindness, and your generous comprehension, and that if any *good* distinction ever attaches to my name, I shall be proud to acknowledge my connection with this place — if any *bad* one, I shall keep silent.

Faithfully and cordially yours,

Thomas Wolfe

P.S. Will you please treat this as a *personal* communication?

---

* Desmond Powell, at present on the staff of the University of Arizona and editor of the *Arizona Quarterly Review*, suffered an attack of tuberculosis while a member of the Washington Square College Department of English.

Friday

[February 27, 1930]

Dear Professor Watt: I gave the talk on The American novel to-night and it seemed to go very well.

A student named _____,[1] who got F in Eng. 35 last term, wants to know if he can take 36 with Mr. Krauss,[2] and be given an examination later in 35. His average is 50 or 55%, somewhat better than those of other students who failed. I will consent to it, and I think Krauss will consent to it, but I told him the final decision rested with you.

Yours,

Tom Wolfe

[1] Name deleted.

[2] Russell Krauss, who replaced Wolfe as a teacher in Washington Square College, had been a Rhodes Scholar. He is at present Associate Professor of English in the Montclair State Teachers College, Montclair, New Jersey.

February 27, 1930.

Mr. Thomas C. Wolfe
27 West 15 Street
New York City

Dear Mr. Wolfe:

Your student, Mr. _____[1] may continue this term in English 36 if he wishes to do so but under no circumstances may any student who has received an "F" in any course in the college be granted permission to remove the "F" by make-up examination. The regulations of the Scholarship Committee on this point are very definite and the department cannot, of course, recommend any violations of them. Mr. Krauss should make this matter clear to Mr. _____.[1]

I am glad that you got along so well last Friday night. If you should not be able to go to East Orange for your lecture on May 2, please let me know well in advance of the date. Do come over to the office to see us occasionally.

Cordially yours,

H. A. Watt
Administrative Chairman

[1]Name deleted.

THE WOLFE – WATT CORRESPONDENCE · SUPPLEMENT

NEW YORK UNIVERSITY

OFFICE OF THE CHANCELLOR

WASHINGTON SQUARE, NEW YORK

28 October, 1935

Dear Tom:

As I don't know your present address I am sending this to you in care of Scribner's. But I did want you to see the attached poem about New York University which has just come out in the Year Book of the School of Architecture. It seems to me it really says something. Are you accepting any invitations these days? Some time I want to get you over to dinner with the family if you don't spend twenty-four hours a day writing.

Cordially yours,

Harry W. Chase[1]
Chancellor

Mr. Thomas Wolfe
c/o Charles Scribner's Sons
597 Fifth Avenue
New York, New York

---

[1]Dr. Harry Woodburn Chase, after serving as President of the University of North Carolina (where he knew Wolfe as editor of the undergraduate paper) and President of the University of Illinois, came in 1933 to New York University as its Chancellor.

STRANGE CAMPUS

Strange campus this, strange view
That long forgot old trees, fresh grass;
That looks on walls of rain stained stone
And windows greyed with old rain drops.
No clinging vines, no arbors green
Where tracery hides the hungry sun;
Here are dull streets where lie the dead,
Confused, blue, broken shadows of
Ten thousand tower tops.

Strange campus this, strange view
That knows no Gothic silhouette
Of chapel spire against the dusk
Or halls that haunt the memory.
Here stand these mighty pinnacles
Aglow like candles at a mass,
And there the street lights, far below,
Mark off the pigeon-holes in which
Six million souls are stuffed.

Strange campus this; but here,
No academic solitude
Can lull the youthful consciousness
Nor coax complaisant attitudes.
For here the murmuring march of life
Outstrips the written word's half truth,
Bids measure all that man can do —
All art, all thought, all enterprise,
By things that are — that live.

Strange campus this; and yet,
Something there is of beauty here
Which rises out of living things,
Of work, of noise, of dust, of speed,
Of hope and countless sad defeats,
Of wealth and want, of peace and pain —
That shakes the slumberous mind awake
And swirls the soul in ecstasies
Within this campus strange.

CHARLES SCRIBNER'S SONS

PUBLISHERS

597 FIFTH AVENUE, NEW YORK

October 30, 1935

Dear Chancellor Chase:

Thanks very much for your note and the enclosed poem. I am
sorry to say that I am not working twenty-four hours a day as I feel I
should be, but I hope to get started soon. I had a wonderful vacation
of more than six months which took me all the way from Denmark
to San Francisco, and I am back here now, ready to work, and desperately eager to get at it but somehow I find it terribly hard to
break through my own inertia and get started. I wonder why people
are like that. No one knows better than I that I must work, and that
my life is nothing without work, and yet I do everything in the world
to avoid it — that is, before I get started.

It would be fine to see you and Mrs. Chase again. Won't you let
me know if we cannot get together sometime, and what time would
be convenient for you?

Thank you for sending me the poem. Yes, I think it decidedly
does say something, and is eloquent and true. As time goes on, and
I have been able to get more detachment and perspective on my
years at New York University, I have realized that being there is one
of the most valuable and fruitful experiences of my whole life. I can
think of no other way in which a young man coming to this terrific

city as I came to it, could have had a more comprehensive and stimulating introduction to its swarming life, than through the corridors and classrooms of Washington Square. In April of this year I had the opportunity to revisit the great English university at Cambridge. It is gloriously beautiful, even more so than I had remembered it, but somehow it seemed remote from the life of the world around us, and my thoughts kept going back to Washington Square and to all the eager, swarming, vigorous life I knew there, and it seemed to me without making comparisons, that whatever happens to our universities in the future, Washington Square was somehow closer to reality than Cambridge. So thanks again for sending me the poem.

Goodbye for the present. I hope I shall see you soon. Meanwhile, with all good wishes to you and Mrs. Chase, I am,

Sincerely,

Tom Wolfe

To Chancellor Harry Woodburn Chase